BURNING

Teresa Boyer

LAUREL
POETRY
COLLECTIVE

ACKNOWLEDGMENTS

Some poems in this collection first appeared in the *Minnesota Poetry Calendar*, *Water~Stone*, *ArtWord Quarterly*, *Poetry Motel*, *Realgoodwords*, *Mined*, *The Lucid Stone*, and the anthology *A New Name for the Sun* (Laurel Poetry Collective, 2003).

Special thanks to the following writers for their support and careful attention to the development of this manuscript: Carol Pearce Bjorlie, Annie Breitenbucher, Kirsten Dierking, Ann Iverson, Deborah Keenan, Yvette Nelson, Jim Moore, Kathy Alma Peterson, Marie Rickmyer, Nancy Walden, and Lois Welshons.

———

Li-Young Lee, "Furious Versions," in *City in Which I Love You: Poems* (Rochester, NY: BOA Editions, Ltd., 1991).

Irene Cieraad, ed., *At Home: An Anthropology of Domestic Space* (Syracuse, NY: Syracuse University Press, 1999).

© 2003 by Teresa Boyer
All rights reserved

ISBN 0-9728934-5-8
Library of Congress Catalog Card Number applied for.

Printed in the United States of America

Published by LAUREL POETRY COLLECTIVE,
1168 Laurel Avenue, St. Paul, MN 55104
www.laurelpoetry.com

Book design by Sylvia Ruud

CONTENTS

I. HORIZON

Horizon	9
Mother	10
Stairs	11
War	12
Answers	13
Corn	14
My Father's House	15
Part of the Story	16
House of My Childhood	17
Night	18

II. BURNING

In My Blood	21
Blue-Eyed King	22
Duane	23
Daughter	24

Silence	26
House of the Boyers	27
Burning	29

III. CHANGE OF HEART

February	33
She Was	34
Dental Emergency Brings Woman Closer to Truth	35
Falling	36
The Rescue	37
Window	38
Ice	39
Love Letter	40
Hearts	42
Change of Heart	43

IV. HOME

House in Winter	47
Thanksgiving	48
The Red Chair	49
The Nightgown	50
Closets	51
Keys	52
The House Has Wounds	53
The Last Hour of Daylight	54
At the Equinox	55
Minneapolis	56

Clover	57
The Library	58
Winter	60
Christmas Morning 1999	61
God Lives in Iowa	62
Home	63
Window, Revisited	64

I.
HORIZON

Horizon

Beyond the cool wire mesh
of the screen door
darkness gives way to haze.
My mother has given me away
to the Indians.

She sits in the kitchen
shielded by a bright light,
balancing her checkbook.

I face my future alone:
the thunder of horses
a black cloud forming
on the horizon.

Mother
(Child's View from Behind the Screen Door)

I watch the curve of her back
as she sits out on the stoop,
arms wrapped around her knees,
mesmerized by the turning of the sky,
pregnant with storm.

Gnats and mosquitoes hover
in the faint glow and hum of the streetlight.
The air is heavy and electric,
then silent and still
as a greenish-yellow seeps across the horizon,
brilliant against the cornfields.

She watches,
drawn to the force of life,
wanting to crawl into the sky.

Stairs

A long, red tongue swallows me down
into the land of banished children.

Cold cement ground, wood beam sky,
lightbulb sun on a silver chain.

In the cinderblock forest
crickets chirp a pinched and hollow song.

Rumpelstiltskin is frozen
in the circle of flax-colored pieces.

I was frozen, too,
at the foot of this red river,

mutant crawdads crawling from the deep freeze.
The only way out is up

the backbone of the house
quietly,

ear pressed to the bottom of the door.

WAR

I remember it as a game of patience over skill
turning the cards one by one
passing them between opponents
with no real sense of ownership.
For we were soldiers, not Generals,
and we knew enough to keep our hands busy,
to move swiftly and without question.
On Sunday afternoons
my sisters and I played like this for hours
filling the void the Day of Rest imposed
on our small-town lives,
monitoring the silence that never came easy
at our house, where peace was always
just a lull.

Answers

When they ask you what you want to be
when you grow up, you tell them *teacher* or *nurse*,
those are the answers;
even *boy* is understandable, for a girl
whose father has no son.
What I really wanted was to be
the voice you never see, the one
from TV commercials and public
service announcements, the one
on audiotapes reserved for children
who say *yellow* when the answer is *white*,
and can't keep track of those tricky,
black, always moving hands
on the happy-faced clock.

Corn

Early mornings in summer
my sisters and I would pedal our bikes
across town to the garden.

Dad's note would say
how many dozens we needed
to fill the orders he had negotiated.

Even in morning we'd sweat,
combing the rows of corn, taller than us,
peeling back the green husks.

Strangers would stop
and we'd bag another dozen or two.
This was business, plain and simple.

We got a cut of the profits, but we would never love it
the way he did.
Not enough to rent a lot, buy seed and herbicide,

dig in the dirt, sweat in the sun, and
gag at the slug-like worms that hid in the husks.
Not enough to stop by the side of the road

and wander into some unknown farmer's field,
as he sometimes did,
just to see how the crop was coming along.

My Father's House

This was my father's house.
Firewood stacked against the west side.
It took two to split the logs, two to carry
the stove-sized chunks,
stack them against the house.

Every other cold winter night we three girls
carried the wood to the basement
two loads each.
We made up stories about Victor and Luigi,
imaginary dead rats that lived in the woodpile.

This was the way we numbed the intolerable cold,
and laughed with our father
unreachable and drunk in his green chair.

Part of the Story

The lies he told to the three little girls
were only part of the story.

The children feared the wolf.
They grieved for the father.

They were grateful for the change in scenery.
But even they could see the dark world

they would inherit—
father/wolf, wolf/father.

House of My Childhood

Pterodactyl at sleep,
beak folded under one wing,
the house is heavy, obstinate,
would screech
at the slightest provocation.
Even in sleep it is wary,
ever ready
to counter-
attack.

Night

Night is grief and the grief is wanting, wanting of rest. My father shuts the door to his room and on restless feet I rise to check the stove again. The dials match up so the house is safe. I sleep, but I never feel safe in this house, pink house with scarred walls that births me over and over in its song of grief. As a child I wake my mother by standing over her bed, staring into her face. Each time, gasping and startled she looks at me like I am not her child, like I am not of this world. One night I wake her by calling, a whisper grown into a plea, but I am no longer a child. Death is standing at the foot of my bed and it has no face. The cloak in the shape of something human is only darkness. I know it, but I have no faith. My mother rescues me. I plead with her to sell the house, I cannot live with the evil the house contains. She cannot hear me. Silent is the night and the night is infinite. I am born there and I am dead there. At sixteen I break out in a rash. Every part of my body is dotted with pink, scaled sores. The doctor tells me to bathe in a solution of tar every night, followed by a second bath in clear water. Each night for a month I lie in the brown water, my body swallowed by the foul smell until the smell becomes a comfort. And each night I sit in a clear bath. Repeatedly tarnished and purified, the sores on my body heal. I give in to the night and the night carries me. In the pages of a book, between the lines, I understand sex for the first time. I recognize desire as something connected with my body, an unmistakable response, at once acknowledged and denied, cast into the pit of not feeling. I feel nothing. Night embodies my hunger, my emptiness. Wild, enraged with storm, the window panes rattle so furiously I am afraid they will shatter. Burrowed deep in my bed I am plotting my escape. I am in the kitchen and the house is burning. I started the fire and I am watching it burn. My father is angry because he will not have his lunch. In his house I am unable to serve him and I will never be able to serve him again. All is consumed until morning rebuilds it again and I am praying for night.

II.
BURNING

*the teller survives
by his telling; by his voice
brinking silence does he survive.*

—Li-Young Lee,
    "Furious Versions"

In My Blood

My blood is the blue blood
of laborers, blue like the shirt
my father wore each day to work.
Work is in my blood,
the kind of work you suffer
to achieve—scrubbing the floor
on hands and knees, hauling
wet laundry to hang on the line,
canning and freezing enough
vegetables to get through winter.
Mending with a needle and thread
is in my blood.
Blood, like a red thread.
Blood of the oppressed, without
enough sense to know they are beaten.
Like weeds that way.

Blue-Eyed King

I see you raging,
Blue-eyed king.
Damn us all
For your frustration.
You pocket our souls
And lecture us on apathy.

I see twenty tired years, spent,
Trying to maintain
Four daughters, and no son,
In a house too small,
In a town you hate,
Pretending to believe.

I long to run
As away, as far, and as fast
As I can,
But yours are the shoes
By the back door waiting.
You are always the one
Who threatens to leave.

I see in your eyes
The pain-streaked tears
Of before, and again,
And again
Our love will never be enough.
We are all afraid
That we will never be free.

Duane

The contents of his work space labeled
in his tiny, precise print: *gun powder, primer, shells.*

He wrote letters to his daughter in college,
a duty learned when his brothers went to Vietnam.

The Armed Forces wouldn't take him,
hearing loss from working around farm machinery.

At Smith & Wesson he learned to build a gun,
earned a license to make and sell ammunition.

Loaded on whiskey, he's in a fighting mood,
"Hey, Ugly!" he grinds his teeth, "I'm gonna *pow* you."

He can't remember what he said last night,
but he can recite poetry memorized in childhood.

On the farm his father worked
him and his brothers like slaves.

No sons of his own, he hides out in his garage,
installed telephone and heat.

He leaves notes on the kitchen table,
small strokes in black ink: *Gone to Hudson. Trim the lawn.*

A man who makes his own war, Teresa,
will never find peace.

DAUGHTER

On the day she was born her father claimed
her with his heart—Teresa Joy,
sweet baby girl.

A covenant passed between them.
I will live through my children, it said.
*As long as I am living, you will have a place
to sleep, food in your mouth.
You are my child; serve me well.*

She turned out
imaginative and fierce,
qualities he admired, but couldn't have

in a daughter,
so he whipped her with a leather belt.
She did not cry, but stared back at him.

She was a good daughter.
He said, *No one will love you but me.*
And she denied herself love.

She left home again and again,
for the city, the mountains, the sea.
It was the city

that bothered him the most.
She lives alone and no one should live
alone in the city.

When he calls late at night,
the tremble of liquor in his voice,
she says, *Yes, Dad. Yes, I understand.
I am the daughter you claimed at birth.*

Your future lives in me.
I will carry the shadow of silenced child as long as you are living.
The woman you cannot see is strong
and knows the truth: The future depends on the other child,
imaginative and fierce.

Silence

I move like a shadow through my neighborhood
up the small hill then down toward the lake
over sidewalks that buckle, crumble, are worn away.
Sun filters down through the trees.
In my path are tiny, pink petals,
each one a silence,
a prayer for a better life.

I'm wearing the weight of silence this spring.
It feels like a magnet
pulling me deeper inside myself.
I'm remembering my family in a way
that makes me want them to be dead.
No more reminders of what we are capable of.
No more spell of loyalty.

Silence is the bargain I made to get this life.
I thought happiness would be easier.
I thought if I went far enough away
I would be changed.
But all along my hands were carriers of violence,
my body, a vessel for disgrace.

House of the Boyers

In the book that traces our family
to before the Civil War,

I follow the French, then German, then
American men—reclaiming the French

name Boyer—to where they settled
in Pennsylvania, then Missouri.

James and Ella look like heads of a lineage
on their wedding day. The somber photo

taken in the house James built for her.
He seated, her standing by his side,

her hand on his shoulder.
Dressed in ordinary clothes

they are looking the same direction,
ahead and away from the camera.

What went wrong? The book doesn't say
why their 14 children moved away;

why James, at 72, burned down the house
and killed himself with strychnine in the barn;

why his wife of 47 years died later that same year,
but was buried in a separate cemetery.

This is the house of the Boyers:
the stumble and scatter of each generation,

desperate acts of escape.
My name is printed there—Teresa,

daughter of Duane, son of Ledru,
son of Clayborn, son of James.

Outside my window, a fading pink
and blue sky blackens

the tree's bare branches
until the light has gone completely,

sparing no one.
Fragile fissures reaching out

and up.

> *But, no one*
> *can tell without cease*
> *our human*
> *story, and so we*
> *lose, lose.*
> —Li-Young Lee, "Furious Versions"

BURNING

The story I can't stop
is about a family
that could not survive
itself.
Where a father's footsteps
spelled danger.
Where, with her hands
around her sister's throat,
a girl learned violence
was within her.
Make no mistake,
there is no mending
in this land-locked history.
There is no escape.
The land is flat
for thousands of miles;
the roads in both directions lead
nowhere.
Learn to be silent and sleep
quickly at night.
Try not to see
death in every set of headlights,
the pattern of hopelessness
repeated in the fields.
Somewhere a woman hiding
her bruises.
Somewhere a child praying

for blindness.
And everywhere, cold, cold,
the only burning
set long ago
by one man
upon his own house.

III.
CHANGE OF HEART

February

For days the phone would not ring. Outside the cats were like crazy squirrels unable to find the acorns they had buried. The trees were dead and provided no shade. The lake sat like a bowl of muddy soup. Even the sun was empty. The phone would not ring the way God does not answer prayers sometimes because there is no answer. And there was no God in my heart. No angel watching over me. No way to stop the hallucinations of the soul pushing the body to its death so that it might escape. No way to stop the dreams about evil men dropping coins, children with deformed hands and feet, my own hands embedded with wire. No way to dial the phone, to say Help Me. Feverishly, I started writing letters. Letters of resignation. Apologies. Suicide notes. Letters I would never send. Grasping toward language, toward a voice that might save me, my voice, reaching back across all the days I had abandoned myself. I surrendered to gravity then, knowing that day would come again and I'd be no more prepared and no more able to stop it. Knowing there could be no witnesses, just the awful presence or lack of light bleeding through the curtains.

She Was

Like an animal trapped
in her body, hunched,
unclean, nervous,
not meant to survive,
God's lost sheep,
her own little fiction.

Dental Emergency Brings Woman Closer to Truth

The toothache I had for the past five days won the battle and I went to the dentist, hoping it would be serious enough to dissuade him from lecturing me on where I'd been for the past six years, but not serious enough to require services over $100. They asked me to fill out a history. I was not at all surprised to find they had it narrowed down to a list of questions with yes or no answers.

I moved quickly through the list, checking headaches and thyroid. For the first time mental illness made my list, and I kept going, adding persistent earaches and stomach pain as serious medical problems I've suffered in my life. It was as though the unbearable pain in my mouth pushed the other sources of pain into the light.

There's a voice in my head that won't shut up. It's saying, "This is the box, the transparent box that I live in, that keeps me sexless and safe." But the box is losing its transparency, beginning to show around the edges. I can't keep silent anymore. At night I dream about long, deep kisses, about the touching of two mouths wanting each other. Sometimes I change sexes. It is natural and not at all difficult or dangerous, until I wake up and hide it from myself by not writing it, or not writing it truthfully.

All these notebooks I keep won't stay separate: school, therapy, dreams, letters, all running together. And I wonder if someday someone will try to put the pieces back together to reconstruct my life. Will they know how sorry I am? How I make excuses for myself in the way I hold my body? Or that I crave a kiss the way an addict craves the drug that will make him feel more powerful?

Do I like my smile? That's the answer that will go down in this history. There's no box for "I don't hate it." So, yes, I like my smile. It's a small risk, a risk I am willing to take today.

Falling

In a hallway I first saw visions of my body falling.
I was walking and I saw another version of myself
drop to the floor. I left myself there,
kept walking.

It had nothing to do with the shoes I was wearing.
It was an ordinary hallway.
The railing and small glass panels were not enough
to keep me from falling.

I kept walking, but it was too late.
I had been falling to my death for months, believing
that in death the pieces of myself I had lost
would be reconciled.

The Rescue

I.

When I returned to you
you said, *If you look at me I will bleed.*

If you speak my ears will turn inward.
If you touch me I will scream.

Most days we lay on the bed
and breathed.

You filled a notebook with stories
of injustices and suffering.

We went back in time
to give you what you needed

to change the endings
to grow up, to restore you to your body.

II.

I remember your heart
churning, defiant.

You were not meant to grow up
and yet you grew.

When I returned to rescue you.

Window

With every name my father cast—
stupid, ugly, fat—
I learned to love myself less
and separate,
until I could push myself
into the frame of any window
—a flutter of a heartbeat—
always watching,
never going in or out.

ICE

Trees encased in ice,
Refracting light like the glare from ten thousand diamonds,

Or two small earrings, their tiny glitter
Once transformed me into an object of beauty.

The trees don't know their beauty is dangerous,
How limbs can snap under the weight of ice.

Under the weight of silence my heart bows.
Beauty encased in memory.

The sun will melt the trees' burden.
My silence is lifting.

I will be beautiful again.

Love Letter
to myself

I.
In my dream
our hands exchange stolen paper,
the elevator keeps us separate.
I want to speak in your language;
instead I am Hispanic with black hair,
the same
in every other way.

II.
Sunlight and the suggestion of you:
thumbprint kisses resounding on my skin.

III.
My one desire
is to sleep in the curve of your arm
where I might kiss your wrist in the night,
my cheek on the pulse of veins that feed your beautiful fingers.
I don't know about love lines, life lines,
but in the soft creases of knuckle,
the smooth warm center of your palm
I am defined.

IV.
Behind these hands
spread like shattered glass
you are duplicated and magnified:
you. you. you.

V.
Surely you are descended from queens,
the elegant casing of ribs, backbone,
prominent collarbone,
the slender line of your neck,
the delicate carriage of hips,
shoulder blades rising like armor,
like wings.

Hearts

hearts are cowards
constantly having affairs
swooning at the mere suggestion of salt or chocolate

hearts have good manners
turtle doves in cashmere
they sing the blood rhyme two and four

they do not fret
over destiny
like the uterus, the brain

in their addictive pulse
hearts never swerve
from their job of moving blood

urgency blooms through them like fists,
cities littered with neon, urine, and cigarettes

Change of Heart

As a girl I wore a lopsided heart
on a chain, the suggestion of love
dropped between my two small breasts

where my duty as a daughter and my desire
to hold a boy's hand
fused me into an infinite loop,

where, in endless trips
around the skating rink, my heart became
my most secret possession.

Now, eighteen years later,
it has decided to shake
its old reputation of

independence at any cost
and wants to love everything—
mangos, God, turbulence.

Delirious,
it begs to be fed,
whispers, *Let's make love in the sun*.

And sun is everywhere,
and on everything.

IV.
HOME

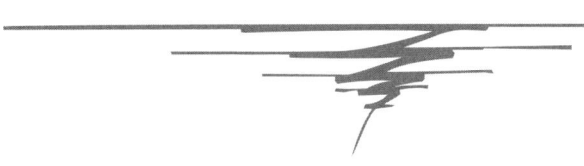

House in Winter

Hunched
like a hen warming eggs
aglow inside
cream colored walls
shimmer.

Thanksgiving

My first Thanksgiving in my own house:
black bean soup with ham,
corn bread muffins and baked sweet potatoes.
I cooked all morning.
Worried when the beans—soaked overnight—
didn't grow, I called home to Iowa
and Dad read me the Menard's ad.
While the soup pot boiled
I set the table with white linens
and marveled at the wealth of china and flatware
in my cupboards: soup tureen, butter dish,
the small butter knife, ladle, large spoons
for soup and dinner forks for the sweet potatoes,
everything down to the salt and pepper shakers.
Michele and baby Isabel arrived
and we talked in the kitchen while the pot boiled
and I mixed bread and rubbed slices of sweet potatoes
with salt and olive oil.
Michele sang to Isabel about a green frog on a log
and later held her hand as we ate so she would sleep,
lulled by the conversation of our daily lives
that has been flowing now for nineteen years,
over a simple meal of soup, that didn't fail.

The Red Chair

In the corner of the dining room
the red chair
is a withdrawn child.

From the secondhand store
six years ago, I chose her
worn color, missing rung, seven spindles.

She reminds me
of my need
for hiding places.

When I cross the room
it comforts me
to see her there.

The Nightgown

The nightgown hangs
by two thin straps.
Sleek as a panther
it dreams of the prowl.
Planning precise movements
through the dark.
Longing for a body.
Momentum.
The power to resist.
Hungry for an equal
but opposite force
the nightgown waits.
It watches
through the closet door
the sliver of light
that grows and fades
that starves without diminishing
the nightgown's desire
to escape
its solitary life.

Closets

My house is rich with closets: twelve hollow chambers blessed with shelves and rods and hooks, doors with glass knobs or a simple metal latch. The coat closet welcomes, relieves my burden of wool, and from a small door inside where it drops through the slot, mail waits to be redeemed. In the hall linen closet, towels and sheets dream of hot baths and overnight guests, among soft rolls of toilet paper, lightbulbs in cardboard nests, Q-tips and cotton balls. The slim broom closet keeps bucket, broom, and mop ever ready for service. Bedroom closets harbor jackets, shoes, and plastic-sheathed party dresses. The attic closets with exposed beams, children's graffiti, and a sign for millwork by Snell Sash and Door offer all that was lacking in the androgynous closets of my childhood—all equal in size with hollow paneled doors that stored little more than family photos in a cardboard box and my father's polyester leisure suits. Even the basement closets bring joy—whole countries of space I have not yet imagined. The workshop with its wall of grey drawers and peg board. Every day these worlds open by my hand and close again to be rediscovered.

Keys

Walking down the street or to the car
my fingers seek the bulk of metal
then the square, flat shape of the house key,
the oblong key to the garage,
the plastic-headed car key,
work key, desk key,
key to my grandfather's trunk
or the suitcase I use when I travel;
keys I carry everywhere:
gold keys, flat keys,
keys with *Do Not Duplicate* inscribed,
keys marked *Titan*,
large keys, cold keys,
keys to a life of scattered and precious things.

The House Has Wounds

The house has wounds
I have felt with my hands.

I don't know how or why,
don't need to know

more than the jagged
and razor-thin scars afford.

The house shelters me
and I warm her walls with paint

build fires in the hearth,
bathe in a blue oasis

based on the floor's original tile.
The house inspires me

to live in comfort. To soothe
the scars no one can see.

The Last Hour of Daylight

On the bed
a pool of yellow light
calls my body
into its holiness.

At the Equinox

I cast on stitches to set the pattern
for needles to follow,
soft blue cotton yarn
for Alexandra, six months old.
My hands work the row
then double back to the beginning,
the way I cast out into my neighborhood
and am pulled home by the momentum of my body.
The days grow shorter and I am grateful
for cool air, the company of shadows,
whole interiors of houses illuminated
like jack-o'-lanterns.

Minneapolis

This is my second life in the city.
The first time around was for skyscrapers,

the pulse of collective life.
This time I just wanted to feel the curve

of Calhoun, to reclaim
the moment I first saw sailboats,

white poles bobbing in the moonlight—
a flock of exotic birds.

Clover

I walk to the park to photograph flowers and fountains.
In the strong morning light, the world glistens;
the sun touches me the way a mother touches the face of her child.

I remember then, this smell of wet grass
mornings my mother carried me, half-asleep, across the lawn,

a memory long gone with its feeling of protection,
stories about dew fairies and the luck of the four-leaf clover
I kneel to photograph.

The Library

for Jim Moore

Crowned in green
its promise of books,
a card catalog I haven't yet searched
lure me
three blocks from the Palmer House Hilton
to the seventh floor
past the Literature and Language Information Desk
to poetry: PS3563
.0618N4
Moore, James
The New Body
1975.

I sit on the floor and open
the small white hard cover,
index card still in the book's front pocket
with a place to stamp the due date and borrower's name—
a sight that makes me momentarily nostalgic
for Mrs. Hoskins and her black ink pad.
I read poem after poem about prison and kittens,
distance and borders, listening intently
to the intimate voice of a friend before I knew him.

I would have been seven when the book came out
sitting on the floor of the school library, reading *Amelia Bedelia*,
or browsing the shelves of the Orange City Public Library
where I spent so much time after school and in summer
that I was there when I started my first period.
Where my fingers scanned the spines
pausing long enough on *Catcher in the Rye*
to consider it, open it, and fall instantly and forever
in love with Holden Caulfield.

Today a poem about doors is the treasure I will take away
copying it carefully into my notebook.
I return the book to its shelf, exit the library,
renewed, buoyant, ready to return
to the noisy, unfamiliar streets of Chicago.

Winter

We rise in darkness.
We shuffle home.
It is a song
that muffles our hearts.

We are weary,
but we love winter—
the lightness of snow,
the heat of our bodies under our coats.

Christmas Morning 1999

Every day should begin like this
the sharp intake of breath,
radiant snow cover melding field and barn and sky.

Hark the Herald Angels Sing rises from me.
Frost melts on the windshield
as I begin the drive from sister to sister,

distance that was once a narrow hallway,
a space between twin beds,
the sound of breathing.

The holiday brings us together
the way snow unites the landscape,
to resume our collective task of memory.

But the snow will melt before the day is done,
before the sun behind her white veil crosses the sky
and we return to our constellation—

distant points connected by voice, pulse.

God Lives in Iowa

God lives in Iowa.
Driving south on Highway 60
I see him sometimes.
He is painting fields green.
He is singing.

Home

The best peach I ever ate
was driving out of Denver,
mountains behind me,
their chipmunks, their hot springs.

That day I wrapped my sunburned body
in the car and let go of everything I owned,
relieved to give in to the magnetic pull
that grounds me to the prairie.

I pulled by the side of the road and wept,
thanking God for beans and corn,
for sisters and homes
to go back to.

Under that enormous sky
all the summers I had lived
seemed possible again.

> [In Dutch paintings of women in the home] *the sexual status of a woman is indicated not only by the condition of the window pane or by its veiling with a curtain, but also in the locking or unlocking of the window.*
> —Irene Cieraad, *At Home: An Anthropology of Domestic Space*

Window, Revisited

It's said that in Dutch paintings
a woman's virtue is reflected in the window she graces.

It's hard not to jump to conclusions
having grown up with all those lace-

curtained windows, the town's false store fronts,
my own personal wooden shoes and tulip hats.

Outside the night song of crickets mixed with traffic
matches the night song I listened to then,

when my bedroom windows seemed to be
the only thing between the evils of the world and home—

evil simply portrayed by triangular shadows
from the window's half-drawn curtains,

shadows that spun around the room
with each passing car.

Now I am a woman
sleeping near a window

fully curtained and open
to the night.

Burning is TERESA BOYER's first collection of poetry. This story of struggle and redemption explores the impact of family, depression, and coming of age in her ultimate quest to find a place called home. Teresa is also the author of *Nursery Rhyme Knits* (Lark Books, 2003), a collection of knitwear designs that incorporate her passions for poetry and knitting. She received her M.F.A. in writing from Hamline University. Teresa lives in Minneapolis.

LAUREL POETRY COLLECTIVE

A gathering of twenty-three poets and graphic artists living in the Twin Cities area, the Laurel Poetry Collective is a self-funded collaboration dedicated to publishing beautiful and affordable books, chapbooks, and broadsides. Started in 2002, its four-year charter is to publish and celebrate, one by one, a book or chapbook by each of its twenty-one poet members. The Laurel members are: Lisa Ann Berg, Teresa Boyer, Annie Breitenbucher, Margot Fortunato Galt, Georgia A. Greeley, Ann Iverson, Mary L. Junge, Deborah Keenan, Joyce Kennedy, Ilze Kļaviņa Mueller, Yvette Nelson, Eileen O'Toole, Kathy Alma Peterson, Regula Russelle, Sylvia Ruud, Tom Ruud, Su Smallen, Susanna Styve, Suzanne Swanson, Nancy M. Walden, Lois Welshons, Pam Wynn, Nolan Zavoral.

For current information about the series—including broadsides, subscriptions, and single copy purchase—visit:

www.laurelpoetry.com

or write:

Laurel Poetry Collective
1168 Laurel Avenue
St. Paul, MN 55104